Brian Wildsmith

Give a Dog a Bone

Oxford University Press

Oxford Toronto Melbourne

This is the story of
a poor stray dog.
She had no home and
she had no bone.
One day she met a
rich poodle.
'I'd love a bone like
that,' said Stray.

But then . . .
MIAOW . . . MIAOW!
WOOF! WOOF!

TWITCH, TWITCH
went her nose outside the
butcher's shop. In she went,
and out she ran with another
bone, bigger and better than
the first one.

So Stray walked on, on and on.
CLATTER, CLATTER,
CLATTER 'Could that be
bones?' Stray wondered.

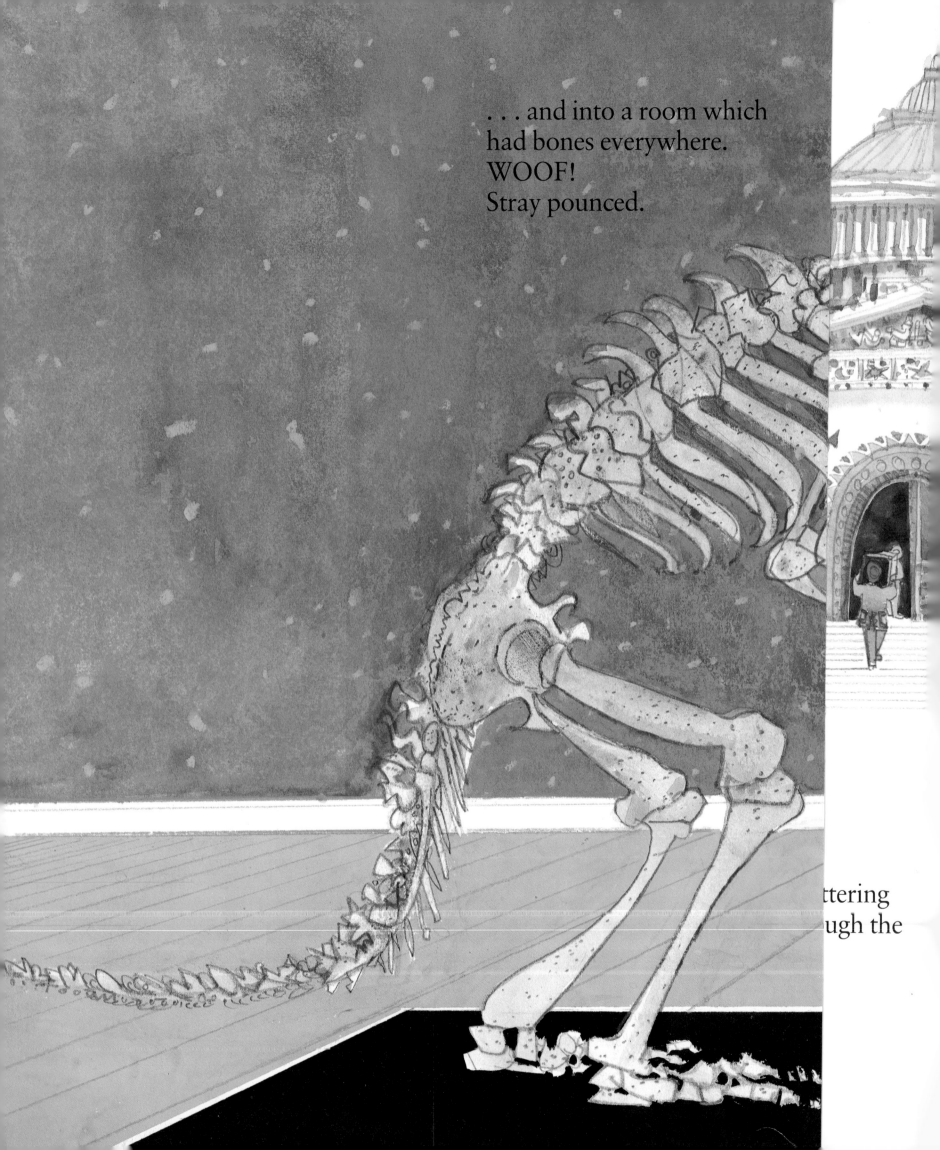

. . . and into a room which
had bones everywhere.
WOOF!
Stray pounced.

ttering
ugh the

Stray raced along the hall and
down some stairs.
SNIFF, SNIFF.
'Do I smell a bone?' Stray
thought.

'STOP!'
oo fast.

She ran out into the road.
'Here's a place to dig.
I'll hide this bone,' she said.

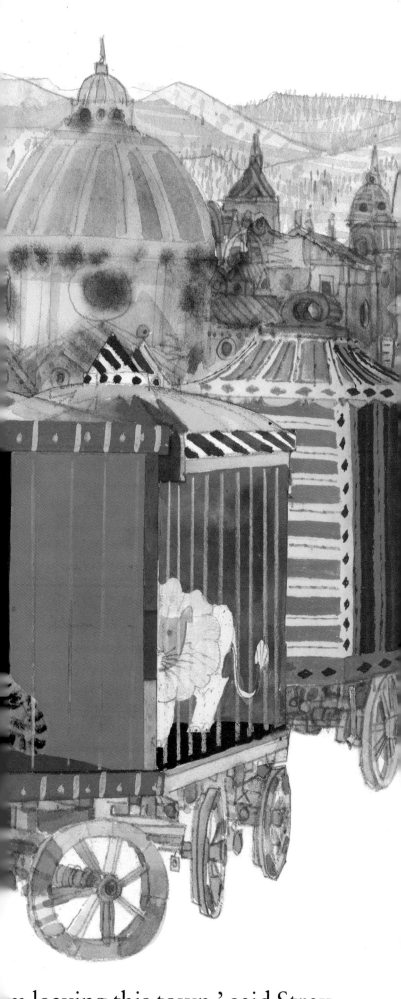

'...m leaving this town,' said Stray.
'...A-RA TA-RA, BOOM DE BOOM!'
...ong came the circus with lions
...d tigers and trumpets blowing . . .

. . . and a nice big bone.

GR-GROARRR! growled the tiger.
But Stray took the bone anyway.

'Here's somewhere
nice and quiet to
eat my bone in,'
said Stray.

Stray walked sadly away
from the fairground and out
of town . . .
DING DONG, DING DONG.
'Just look at those bones,'
said Stray.

CLICK, CLICK.
'I'll just have a quiet chew . . .'

'NEIGH, NEIGH
snorted the horses. And Stray jump
on as the carriage rolled awa

. . . where they all lived happily ever after.

For all Strays,
two-legged
and
four-legged

Oxford University Press, Walton Street, Oxford OX2 6DP

Oxford London
New York Toronto Melbourne Auckland
Kuala Lumpur Singapore Hong Kong Tokyo
Delhi Bombay Calcutta Madras Karachi
Nairobi Dar es Salaam Cape Town

and associated companies in
Beirut Berlin Ibadan Mexico City Nicosia

Oxford is a trade mark of Oxford University Press

© Brian Wildsmith 1985
First published 1985
ISBN 0 19 279814 6

British Library Cataloguing in Publication Data
Wildsmith, Brian
Give a dog a bone.
I. Title
823'.914[J] PZ10.3
ISBN 0–19–279814–6

Typeset by Oxford Publishing Services
Printed in Hong Kong